EVERYBODY'S
BEST FRIEND

Written by **Larry Dane Brimner** • Illustrated by **Christine Tripp**

For my friends at Brooks Elementary
—L.D.B.

For Julie, who always believed in and encouraged me
—C.T.

Library of Congress Cataloging-in-Publication Data

Brimner, Larry Dane.
  Everybody's best friend / written by Larry Dane Brimner ; illustrated by Christine Tripp.
    p. cm. — (Rookie choices)
  Summary: While the Corner Kids are giving their dog Jake a bath, they recall when Three J
first got Jake and how he decided to share him with Gabby and Alex.
  ISBN 0-516-22542-1 (lib. bdg.)   0-516-27791-X (pbk.)
  [1. Dogs—Fiction. 2. Sharing—Fiction.] I. Tripp, Christine, ill. II. Title. III. Series.
  PZ7.B767 Ev 2002
  [E]—dc21

                              2001008235

This book is about **sharing**.

The Corner Kids were giving
Jake a bath. They scrubbed
and rubbed. They rubbed
and scrubbed.

Then Jake shook.

"Yikes!" the Corner Kids said.
Jake always soaked everyone
when he had a bath.

Three J, Gabby, and Alex called themselves the Corner Kids because they lived on corners of the same street. Jake was the dog they shared.

Gabby nuzzled Jake's wet nose. "Remember when we first got him?" she asked.

It had been a sunny Saturday last spring. Three J's dad had taken him to the animal shelter to pick out a dog. Gabby and Alex had gone, too.

Three J found Jake right away.
"This is the one," he said. Jake
was wagging his tail so hard that
his whole body wiggled. He was
licking Three J's face.

Three J giggled and said, "You guys should get dogs, too."

Gabby sighed. "Abuela says we don't have room for a dog."

Alex nodded. "My mom says we can't afford one."

"A dog is a big responsibility," said Three J's dad. "You have to walk him and feed him. You have to give him baths. You have to give him lots of attention."

"I'll do those things," Three J said. "We'll be best friends."

"I thought the three of *us* were best friends," Gabby said.

Three J didn't know what to say.

19

Then Three J's dad said, "You will have to figure out something for Tuesdays and Thursdays after school. Jake won't be able to come with us to visit Grandma."

On the ride home that day, everyone was quiet. Three J thought about what his father had said about visiting his grandma without Jake. He thought about Gabby and Alex. They were both sad.

23

Then Jake jumped from the front seat to the back seat. He landed right in Gabby's lap, and Gabby started laughing. So did Alex.

That gave Three J an idea. "Why don't we share Jake?" he asked.

Gabby and Alex didn't understand.

"He can live with me," Three J said. "On Tuesday and Thursday afternoons Jake can stay with you. That way he'll be *our* friend, not just mine."

Everybody liked the sound of that.

ABOUT THE AUTHOR

Larry Dane Brimner studied literature and writing at San Diego State University and taught school for twenty years. The author of more than seventy-five books for children, many of them Children's Press titles, he enjoys meeting young readers and writers when he isn't at his computer.

ABOUT THE ILLUSTRATOR

Christine Tripp lives in Ottawa, Canada, with her husband Don; four grown children—Elizabeth, Erin, Emily, and Eric; son-in-law Jason; grandsons Brandon and Kobe; four cats; and one very large, scruffy puppy named Jake.